I0626961

AFTER THE TOUR

GUIDING YOUR PROSPECTS FROM *Interest to Action*

KIERA DESCHAMPS

For more information, visit www.kdconsults.com/

Kiera DesChamps
CEO/Founder KD Consulting Group, LLC

ISBN: 979-8-9995485-0-4 (paperback)
ISBN: 979-8-9995485-1-1 (eBook)

Library of Congress Control Number: 2025915283

Cover Design by Courtney Williamson
Interior Design by Amit Dey

TABLE OF CONTENTS

ACKNOWLEDGMENTS

To the active adult and senior living operators: Thank you for allowing me to learn from your expertise, your challenges, and your openness. To those who welcomed me into your communities and shared your insights freely, I am truly grateful. To those who overlooked my calls, emails, or messages, I thank you as well. Your silence helped to reinforce for me the importance of this work and pushed me to write a book that brings value and opens doors for deeper connection. If you're reading this now, I'm glad we've found a moment to connect, and I hope we'll partner soon.

To my industry colleagues: Thank you for welcoming me into this space. I've had the pleasure of meeting people who began as "deal friends" and became real friends. You've taught me the inner workings of this industry, introduced me to innovation, and reminded me that none of us does this work alone. We are part of a community grounded in compassion and collaboration.

To the many clients I've had the honor of serving over the past decade: Thank you for inviting me into your homes and lives during one of the most vulnerable times. Thank you for your honesty, your trust, your laughter, and your stories. I carry your words and your courage with me. Some of you even adopted me as your honorary grandchild, and those relationships are among my greatest gifts.

And to my friends and family: I can already hear you saying, "It's about time, Kiera!" You've championed me from the start—pushing me forward, lifting me up, and reminding me that this calling has always been within me. Thank you for your prayers, your patience, and your unwavering love. You remind me daily that God continues to order my steps, and fear has no place in that journey. I love you deeply and forever.

To my husband, Louis: *Thank you for always believing in me and giving me the space to build. Your endless love and support, no matter what direction I choose, is one of the greatest blessings of my life. This journey would not have been possible without you.*

PREFACE

In today's competitive senior living and active adult market, having the best amenities, floor plans, and marketing campaigns isn't enough. After the Tour, when the excitement fades and the logistics kick in—that's when the real decision-making begins. And too often, that's where prospects stall... or walk away.

In *After the Tour*, Kiera DesChamps reveals the overlooked moments that determine whether a lead becomes a resident. With over a decade of experience working alongside operators, sales teams, and families in transition, she offers a powerful, practical, and deeply human approach to sales that goes beyond the script.

You'll learn how to:

- Recognize the emotional and logistical cues your prospects are already giving you
- Transform vendor lists into trusted partnerships that accelerate move-ins
- Equip your sales team with tools to guide—not pressure—prospects forward
- Reduce your conversion costs by removing the true barriers to commitment

- Use her LEADer model to deliver a full-circle, relationship-based experience

Whether you're a sales director, executive leader, adult child, or aging adult making your own decisions, this book will challenge you to rethink what happens after the handshake and beyond the tour. This book is your guide to becoming not just a better closer, but a trusted partner in one of life's biggest transitions.

Because the sale doesn't end with a walkthrough—it starts when someone finally feels ready to move forward.

INTRODUCTION

"**H**ey, *Kiera. We are planning a girls' trip to Florida. Come with us!*" This question was asked by a group of my best friends right after my three-year contract ended at a higher education institution. I felt guilty even considering this trip, especially since I was newly unemployed, even though my husband was in full support of me going. To generate some guilt-free income, I decided to drive for Uber. This was, hands-down, the best job that I ever had. Even though I only worked for about four to six weeks, I had a blast. I met so many new people, discovered eateries and neighborhoods around Charlotte, and I was my own boss. Like most rideshare drives, the passenger normally sits in the backseat. On one particular morning, my rider decided to sit up front with me. On our twenty-five-minute drive to her destination, she asked the usual questions, *"how long have you been a driver, do you like it, what is next for you, etc.?"* I then learned that she owned a small senior move management company that helped support active and older adults, and their families, transition to a community or development. She asked me if I would be interested in helping support her business with marketing and development for a few hours a week. This was my first exposure to the active and older adult industry. My goal was to make a few extra dollars to go on a girls' trip and help a small business until I found my "real job." Since then, I have spent ten years working in the industry as a bridge of support between communities and their future residents.

This book was written from a place of proximity. I've sat at dining room tables surrounded by moving boxes. I've listened to overwhelmed adult children trying to do right by their parents. I've worked alongside sales teams doing their best to balance performance goals with genuine care. And I've watched communities lose move-ins—not because the product wasn't right, but because the process was incomplete.

That's why I created the LEADer model—a framework designed to coach and empower leaders to guide their prospects through the entire transition journey. It's not just about tracking leads and delivering tours. It's about asking the right questions, listening for logistical cues, and recognizing emotional hesitation before it becomes a barrier.

The LEADer model is rooted in the belief that when we follow the lead of our prospects—by observing, guiding, and owning every step of the process—we not only close more sales, we create more trust. This book is your invitation to embrace a more holistic approach to sales. One that equips you to take ownership not just of your role, but of the entire experience your future residents are stepping into.

Whether you are a senior living sales VP, a sales counselor, or a community operator—this book was written for you.

Let's shift the way we serve, one meaningful conversation at a time.

— Kiera DesChamps

PART ONE

YOUR PROSPECT

1

UNDERSTANDING YOUR PROSPECT

"I want to age in a place where I feel supported, but not limited," shared a recent 68-year-old client touring an active adult community.

I first discovered this industry about ten years ago, and the more I learned about the aging population, the more I realized how close I am to entering this stage of life myself. By the time you read this book, I will be fifty-two years old—just a few short years from fifty-five, the threshold of my "active adult" era. While I am grateful for every day, I also recognize how much I still don't know, and that uncertainty can be daunting. How do I prepare? Am I ready?

My background yields from the people-helping industry in professional counseling, therapeutic counseling, higher education, and consulting. I feel as if my life has come full circle and every experience was perfectly designed to bring me here today. I have worked with many people beginning with at-risk youth, to now working in the aging adult living industry. One thing I've learned in this industry is that there is a vast amount of information to navigate. For those without direct experience or exposure, it can feel overwhelming to figure out where to start. For those of you who have just entered the industry, welcome. For the veterans reading this book, I am happy that we can do this together.

Early in my career in the professional move management industry, I was simply excited to be allowed into a community to drop off collateral. Just being a referral partner felt like a win; getting past the front gate was an accomplishment in itself! I could write another book on the many creative ways that I was able to get past either the front gate keepers, or the front desk employees…but I can't give away all my business secrets. As I toured more communities, engaged with sales teams, and attended industry conferences, I quickly realized that if I wanted to make a real impact, I needed to transition from simply being a referral partner to becoming a trusted business partner. That meant understanding the business, identifying pain points, and offering real solutions. A true value-added partnership.

As the aging population continues to grow, it is crucial to understand the demographic trends, expectations, and outlook of this group. The next decade will bring significant shifts in how Baby Boomers approach retirement, housing, and lifestyle decisions, shaping the future of senior living communities and services needed. Today's active and aging adults are redefining what it means to grow older. This cohort includes individuals typically aged fifty-five and older, but their lifestyles, values, and needs are more diverse than ever. Many are still working part-time, traveling, volunteering, caregiving for a spouse or grandchild, or exploring second careers. They are tech-savvy, independent, and prioritize purpose, wellness, and convenience. They are adjusting, adapting, and evolving to the changes.

Demographics & Population

The aging population in the U.S. and globally is expanding rapidly due to increased life expectancy and aging Baby Boomers.

- **Population Growth:** By 2030, all Baby Boomers will be at least sixty-five years old, with the senior population expected to exceed 120 million in the U.S. (U.S. Census Bureau, 2020). Boomers make up just 21 percent of the U.S. population—but hold over 50 percent of the nation's wealth. That's more than $96 trillion in purchasing power.

- **Longevity Trends:** Advances in healthcare and lifestyle changes mean people are living longer, often well into their eighties and nineties. According to the National Institute on Aging (NIA), the number of Americans aged eighty-five and older is projected to triple by 2050.

- **Diverse Backgrounds:** They come from diverse cultural, economic, and professional backgrounds, making their needs and preferences more varied than ever. The Pew Research Center notes that by 2035, older adults will outnumber children for the first time in U.S. history.

As this population grows, so do the expectations for housing, wellness, and community engagement. Here are key trends for us to watch over the next decade:

- **Active Aging & Wellness-Focused Living:** More people are prioritizing physical fitness, mental wellness, and social engagement over traditional retirement lifestyles (World Health Organization, 2022). A growing segment are solo agers—adults without immediate family to rely on.

- **Desire for Customization:** The "one-size-fits-all" model of senior living is shifting toward more personalized living arrangements, including hybrid and intergenerational communities.

- **Technology Integration:** Smart home features, telehealth, and AI-driven wellness tracking are becoming standard expectations (AARP, 2022).

- **Aging in Place vs. Community Living:** While some want to remain in their homes, many are choosing senior communities that offer services to maintain independence longer (National Institute on Aging, 2023). Many are downsizing by choice, not necessity, looking for lifestyle enhancement, not care. The average person moving into the active adult community is sixty-seven years old.

- **Financial Preparedness:** Future seniors will have different financial challenges and expectations, requiring more flexible pricing models and innovative financial planning options (Harvard Joint Center for Housing Studies, 2021).

One of the biggest hurdles for those considering a transition to a community is the physical and logistical challenge of moving. Many have lived in their homes for decades, accumulating not just belongings but also emotional attachments.

Sorting through years of possessions can be overwhelming, requiring emotional and practical support. Many need to sell their homes before they can transition into an active adult or senior living community. Understanding real estate trends, timing, and financial implications is critical. Additionally, packing, hiring movers, and setting up a new home can be physically and mentally exhausting.

I find that communities that offer vetted and trusted resources to assist with these logistical challenges provide a major advantage in helping older adults make a smooth transition. Gaining support in navigating these obstacles will significantly lower stress.

The landscape will continue evolving, with a strong emphasis on:

- **More Housing Options:** Expect growth in active adult communities, co-housing models, and mixed-use developments tailored to older adults.

- **Greater Focus on Social Connection:** Communities will invest in engagement programs, lifelong learning, and travel opportunities to combat loneliness (National Institute on Aging, 2022).

- **Expanded Health and Wellness Programs:** Wellness will be a priority, with more communities offering fitness classes, mental health support, and nutrition programs. Communities are being conspicuously built within established neighborhoods with walkability.

- **Increased Demand for Concierge Services:** Transportation, concierge services, and technology support will be key amenities.

- **Greater Integration of Transition Assistance:** The most successful communities will not only sell a lifestyle but also actively assist in downsizing, home sales, and move coordination (Senior Housing News, 2023). They are offering guided support and turnkey concierge services that move prospects forward.

Understanding the changing needs of the aging population is essential for shaping the future of senior living. With increased longevity, a greater emphasis on active aging, and evolving housing preferences, the next decade will see a significant transformation in how communities serve this generation.

2
EMOTIONAL AND LOGISTICAL BARRIERS

Did you know that 81 percent of your prospects delay moving due to logistical concerns like downsizing, selling a home, or fear of the transition?

Leaving Home

It was June 20th, 1993, the day after my wedding, which also happened to be Father's Day. Our cars were packed with wedding gifts and last-minute items, ready for the long drive from South Carolina to the panhandle of west Florida. I had just married my husband, a new Airman in the USAF. I'll never forget the way my dad looked as he stood in the yard, waving goodbye. His smile was warm, his eyes held a hint of pride, and a few tears glistened. I glanced back but couldn't linger; my throat tightened, and my own eyes filled with tears. I was leaving home. The place that had been my childhood sanctuary, and the backdrop of my college and familial years. As excited as I was to embark on this new chapter filled with adventure and possibilities, I was also leaving behind something irreplaceable: home. Although I was heading towards something new and exciting, my heart still mourned the loss of what I was leaving behind.

Leaving a home where one has spent decades is an emotional experience. Many older adults associate their homes with cherished memories, making the transition feel like leaving behind a piece of their identity. The home represents a lifetime of experiences, making it emotionally difficult to leave. Many often fear losing the familiarity and comfort they have built over decades.

Moving to a new environment brings uncertainty about social connections, daily routines, and personal independence. This fear can cause hesitation in making a transition decision. Some have strong neighborhood ties and routines that provide a sense of belonging. Leaving behind familiar faces and daily rituals can cause emotional distress. Understanding and addressing the emotional burden of transitioning can significantly ease a client's decision-making process.

"I was afraid I wouldn't fit in, that I'd lose my sense of purpose. It wasn't just a move; it was a whole new way of life. Seriously, I don't know any of these people. I met a few men during tours, but I am not in high school anymore. All of this is just too much change at once." – Robert, seventy-nine, new resident.

Finances are one of the most significant concerns for future residents and their families. The cost of buying a home in an active adult neighborhood, or a suite in a senior living community, varies widely, and many people struggle to understand their financial options. They worry about whether they can sustain this cost of living long-term, particularly as healthcare expenses increase with age. Many rely on the sale of their home to finance their move. The uncertainty of the housing market and the stress of selling can delay the process.

Different communities offer varying pricing structures, such as entrance fees, monthly rent, equity models, and add-on care services. Many families are unaware of financial assistance programs, long-term care insurance, or veteran benefits that can help offset costs. Financial concerns often cause decision paralysis, preventing prospects from committing to a move. By offering financial counseling, providing clarity on pricing structures, and connecting prospects with financial advisors or real estate experts, communities can help eliminate financial uncertainty. Proactively educating families on their options can significantly accelerate move-in decisions.

The actual process of moving is overwhelming, particularly for older adults who have accumulated a lifetime of belongings. Many face physical and logistical barriers that make the transition difficult. Deciding what to keep, donate, or discard is a daunting task that can delay a move. Our prospects often struggle with parting with sentimental items.

Mobility challenges make packing, lifting, and organizing extremely difficult. Without family support, the idea of moving can feel insurmountable. Finding trustworthy movers, setting up new utilities, changing addresses, and handling medical transitions can be overwhelming for older adults who may not be comfortable with technology or modern moving services. The physical and logistical demands of moving often become the biggest roadblocks for active or older adults considering a transition to senior living. Simplifying the transition process can make the move feel less daunting and more achievable.

Moving Stressors:

Logistical Barriers

- Downsizing stress and clutter overload
- Home sale delays or complications
- Lack of trusted move-related vendors
- Anxiety around the moving day itself
- Physical limitations with packing or lifting

Overwhelming List of Decisions

- Choosing the right floor plan and fit
- Understanding financial plans and contracts
- Balancing lifestyle vs. care needs
- Healthcare level confusion
- Vendor list overload with no guidance

Time Crunch & External Pressures

- Sudden health events prompting urgent moves
- Family pressure for quicker decisions
- Lease endings or pending home closings
- Cross-state transitions with no local help
- Unit availability before client readiness

Emotional & Psychological Barriers

- Fear of losing independence
- Guilt or grief from life changes

- Cultural discomfort or underrepresentation
- Shame around clutter, home state, or finances

By recognizing the emotional, financial, and logistical challenges that your customers face, sales and marketing teams can better tailor their approach. Providing proactive guidance and reassurance can ultimately make the transition smoother, leading to increased occupancy rates and resident satisfaction. You already know the barriers, so don't be afraid to talk about the large, smelly elephant in the room.

3
WHY WOULD YOU INVEST?

*Did you know that 63 percent of prospective
residents tour a community at least twice before
making a decision, but many drop off due to lack of
a clear next step?*

A s I continued my discovery in this industry, I immersed
myself by asking questions—lots of them. I wanted
to understand the financial pressures, occupancy challenges, and overarching goals of these communities. One
pivotal moment came when a Director of Sales called me
in a panic, needing eight move-ins within two months.
Because we had built a trusted relationship, she turned
to me for ideas.

One of my first observations was the number of
outdated or empty apartments, which were making it
even harder to attract prospects. Together, we created a
cost-effective plan to refresh these units, organized an
open house to showcase the hard-to-sell apartments,
and created a move-in program. While the community's occupancy was low, they recognized that investing

strategically in these efforts would help accelerate move-ins and meet their goal. Ultimately, the cost of an empty apartment was a far greater financial risk than investing in solutions to fill them. Here is where I positioned myself to become a trusted business partner, not just a referral on a pamphlet. By understanding her pain points we collaborated and built a solution that had a significant financial impact on her community. In case you were wondering, she was able to gain six successful move-ins in the two months following our work.

The industry requires substantial investments in marketing, recruitment, and operational strategy to attract qualified prospects and convert them into residents. Understanding these costs and the critical need to accelerate occupancy is essential for achieving a positive return on investment (ROI).

In today's competitive aging living market, where margins are narrowing and occupancy pressures are increasing, sales and operational leaders must evaluate every decision through the lens of ROI. One often-overlooked area of strategic opportunity is the investment in full logistical support services as part of the move-in process. Beyond amenities and pricing strategies, this approach directly impacts the sales cycle duration and total cost per conversion.

Financial Investment

It is well documented that communities invest heavily in advertising and branding to attract prospective residents. Digital marketing efforts, such as social media campaigns, paid advertising, search engine optimization (SEO), and website development, play a crucial role in generating leads. Traditional print advertising, including brochures, direct mail campaigns, and magazine placements, remains a valuable strategy for reaching targeted demographics. Additionally, community engagement initiatives, such as hosting events, open houses, and sponsorships, enhance visibility and foster relationships with potential residents and their families.

Beyond marketing, sales team and human capital investments are also significant. Salaries and commissions for sales and marketing staff account for a substantial portion of expenses, while ongoing training programs ensure that teams remain knowledgeable and effective in converting leads. Implementing customer relationship management (CRM) systems streamlines the lead-tracking process and enhances communication with prospects.

Further, lead generation costs contribute to overall marketing expenditures. Many communities rely on third-party referral services and placement agencies to identify qualified prospects, while data analytics tools help optimize targeted campaigns and improve conversion rates. By integrating these strategies, communities can maximize their outreach efforts and drive occupancy growth efficiently. My goal is to establish processes that prevent hot leads from becoming cold by creating built-in programs.

Yes, there is a lot of jargon that I mentioned above, so let's look at this in terms of average investments. The average cost per lead in the industry varies depending on the type of care and marketing strategies employed; however, conversion rates indicate that not all leads result in move-ins. The average conversion rate for senior living leads is approximately 30 percent, meaning that a majority of leads do not convert into residents. Hence, the reason for this discussion.

Why Logistics Matter

"When you help solve their biggest worry—the logistics—you don't just win the sale, you earn their trust."

Research shows that one of the most significant emotional and logistical barriers to moving into senior living is not selecting a floor plan or agreeing on pricing—it's the fear and stress surrounding downsizing, selling a home, and relocating. Prospects often delay making a decision because they feel overwhelmed by the process, even when they are emotionally ready for a lifestyle change.

According to the National Association of Senior Move Managers (NASMM, 2023) and myLifeSite, concerns around the downsizing process are frequently cited as one of the leading obstacles to move-in. The National Association of Productivity & Organizing Professional (NAPO, 2024) describes the process as a mental exercise and emotional tide of parting with their belongings. Communities that do not offer structured transition support risk losing warm leads simply because the logistical burden is too high. Trust me, I have been in their homes, sat at their tables, worked in their attics, and dried their tears. This is a painful process that needs support.

This is especially true in the fast-growing fifty-five+ active adult market. These prospects often begin the process independently, sometimes years before they are ready to commit. Many are downsizing from large homes, helping aging spouses, or navigating retirement changes. Because the transition timeline can span many months—or even years—communities that offer logistical planning support and right-sizing guidance from the start are far more likely to retain long-term interest and successfully convert. By the way, the average active adult doesn't move into the active living community until sixty-seven years old.

The ROI of Logistical Incentives

Communities that offer move-in incentives tied directly to transition services (such as floor planning, move management, real estate assistance, or packing services) see measurable results:

- **Accelerated Sales Cycle**: CCRC Growth reports that reducing a typical six-month sales cycle to two months by offering logistical support can save up to $80,000 in marketing and sales labor costs.
- **Improved Lead Conversion**: Senior Housing News (2023) noted that communities offering proactive transition support converted higher-quality leads and reported stronger move-in ratios. Why isn't this a standard practice?
- **Greater Emotional Readiness**: Providing logistical support eases fear and uncertainty, making prospects feel cared for and building trust—an essential factor in high-ticket decision-making.

Consider a community that spends $20,000 a month in marketing. If their sales cycle is six months, they may spend $120,000 before a prospect moves in. Reducing the decision time to two months by offering concierge-level transition support cuts that cost to $40,000, preserving $80,000 in potential margin. This is equivalent to someone's salary.

While competitive incentives like limited-time pricing, move-in specials, and added perks can be effective motivators, they could be positioned as part of a broader strategy rather than the sole selling point. Discounts and upgrades may attract attention, but they don't necessarily move the client forward in the decision-making process; they only add value once the move is complete.

Instead of offering incentives that only activate *after* move-in (like rent discounts or upgrades), communities can front-load value by offering services that move the prospect forward.

Examples include:

- Paying a portion of the client's upfront moving expenses
- Partnering with professional move managers
- Providing space planning and home prep as part of the reservation package. This is my first choice and a highly recommended option for sales teams to offer. It provides the prospect with an immediate vision of living in your community. They get to visualize their furniture in their new home, which raises their comfort level about making the move
- Hosting logistical workshops for prospects and their families

Case Example: Measuring ROI of Logistical Incentives

In a fifty-five+ active adult community, a developer offered an $8,000 move-in incentive package, which covered downsizing assistance, professional space planning, and full-service move management. This initiative helped reduce the sales cycle from six months to three months. As a result, the community reduced its marketing spend from $120,000 to $60,000 over the course of the conversion, while increasing deposits by 18 percent. After accounting for the $8,000 incentive, the community still netted a savings of approximately $52,000 per conversion and moved residents in 50 percent faster.

A CCRC community with entrance fees of $500,000+ implemented a $5,000 incentive that included preferred move managers and pre-move planning. This helped reduce the sales cycle from six to four months. With an average marketing investment of $20,000 per month, the savings in marketing alone was approximately $40,000. Subtracting the $5,000 incentive, the net gain per move-in was around $35,000, and the transition experience added confidence to a high-value sale.

In another case, a rental senior living community offered a $1,500 logistical credit to support packing or moving expenses. This smaller incentive successfully shortened the move-in timeline from ninety to sixty days and helped reduce the risk of vacancy. With fewer delays and less time invested per lead, the community saw a net ROI of over $13,000 per conversion.

These real-life use cases illustrate that strategic upfront investment in transition support not only creates a more seamless prospect experience, it delivers real ROI.

Community Type	Incentive Amount	Sales Cycle Reduced	Marketing Cost Saved	Net Savings per Move-In	Notes
55+ Active Adult	$8,000	6 → 3 months	$60,000	$52,000	Increased deposit rate by 18%
CCRC (Entrance Fee: $500K)	$5,000	6 → 4 months	$40,000	$35,000	Supported high-value entry with concierge logistics
Rental Community (AL/MC)	$1,500	90 → 60 days	~$15,000	~$13,500	Low-cost incentive to avoid extended vacancy

The cost per move-in is a critical metric that reflects the total investment required to secure a new resident. This cost varies widely based on factors such as marketing strategies, community location, and the level of care provided. As a result, prolonged vacancies can significantly impact a community's financial health. Accelerating occupancy is essential to maximize ROI and ensure the sustainability of the community. Vacant units contribute to financial losses due to ongoing operational costs without corresponding revenue.

If operators want to reduce the cost per move-in (which currently ranges between $10,000 to $25,000 or more, according to Senior Housing News), they must view transition support not as a bonus service, but as a core sales and retention strategy. Make it a part of what you do.

What Works:

- Built-in concierge service or a partner who provides this service

- Packing and downsizing assistance
- Floor planning and space design
- Pre-move real estate referrals
- Transition workshops for prospects
- Marketing and retention events that are strategically planned

What Doesn't Work:

- Generic rent discounts with delayed activation
- One-size-fits-all gift cards or merchandise
- A list full of various vendors

Finally, staff training and sales excellence remain critical, as equipping sales teams with a deep understanding of the emotional and logistical barriers prospects face allows for more meaningful, consultative interactions that build trust and drive commitment. We will discuss taking a holistic approach to sales in the next chapters.

By embedding full logistical services into your sales process, you not only increase your community's value proposition, you actively remove the biggest obstacle standing between a prospect and their decision to say yes.

The business case is clear: investing in how people *get there* is just as important as what they'll find once they arrive. This is a marketing plan in itself.

PART TWO

THE DRIVE HOME

4
THE DRIVE HOME AFTER THE TOUR

"I remember when my mother first toured a community. She loved the place, but once we got home, reality set in. What about her things? How would she afford it? Who would help her move? It was overwhelming, and she just shut down."

— Adult Daughter

Transitioning into a new community is one of the most significant life changes an individual or family can face. While a well-conducted tour can spark excitement about the possibilities of a new lifestyle, prospects often find themselves overwhelmed during the drive home. Successful sales and marketing teams understand and take ownership of these emotions, challenges, and logistical hurdles that follow a visit. By addressing these concerns effectively, communities can help prospects navigate their journey with confidence, ultimately leading to quicker and more informed decisions.

Once your future residents leave a tour, reality sets in on their way home. Let's hold space and imagine the long drive home with a head full of information, only to arrive home to face what's next. While they may have been impressed by the amenities, friendly staff, and beautiful surroundings, they must now confront a range of challenges that can stall their decision-making process. Prospects are confronted with what is possible, to what feels impossible. Imagine this overwhelming and daunting feeling of facing the realities of what's to come. Seeing life from the perspective of the client really helps this hit home.

"I had stacks of paperwork from three different communities. I didn't know where to start, so I just set them aside to read when I was ready." – Susan, eighty-two, prospective resident.

Your prospects are inundated with paperwork, legal questions, and family opinions. They are expected to compare services, understand contracts, and weigh future needs—all while emotionally processing a major life change. Sales teams unintentionally overwhelm prospects with options rather than guiding them through clarity.

We already know that moving is a daunting task. It is known as the third most stressful event in a person's life next to death and divorce. Many older adults have spent decades in their homes, accumulating a lifetime of memories and possessions. Downsizing requires time, effort, and emotional resilience. Without a clear action plan, prospects may feel immobilized by the sheer magnitude of the transition.

"I walked through the tour thinking, This is exactly where I want to be. But then I got home and looked around at all my belongings, and I just felt stuck. How do I even begin? It all gives me anxiety." – Mary, seventy-eight, prospective resident.

Often, the decision to move isn't made alone. Adult children, spouses, and other family members play a role in the process. Some may encourage the transition, while others may resist it, fearing change or worrying about financial implications. If family members are not aligned in their support, it can create delays or even prevent a move altogether. Adult children may disagree on what's best, causing delays, or the primary decision-maker isn't always present—or vocal—in the process. One family member might be pushing the move for convenience, while another resists out of emotional loyalty. The list of potential conflicts within the family is long.

Some sales teams rarely receive training to navigate these exact dynamics, yet they comprise a central obstacle to move-in momentum. Even when a prospect sees the value in the move, financial concerns can create hesitation. Many older adults worry about affording monthly fees, selling their homes, or preserving assets for their families. Without clear guidance on financial planning and available resources, they may postpone their decision indefinitely.

Here are some thoughts and emotions they'll never discuss out loud, or at least with the salesperson:

- Feeling guilt over leaving a spouse's memory behind.
- The fear of being judged by family for "giving up" on independence.
- Resentment that no one else in the family is stepping in to help.
- Embarrassment over the state of their current home (clutter, disrepair, incontinence, outdated).

Sales teams often assume hesitancy is about price or timing, when it instead may be grief, shame, or fear of losing control.

Unfortunately, communities invest heavily in marketing strategies to attract prospects, yet there is often a gap in support once the tour is completed. Marketing materials highlight features and lifestyle benefits, but they often fail to address the real-life complexities that arise after a visit. During a tour, prospects receive brochures, pricing details, and vendor lists, but without a structured follow-up process that includes the emotional journey of prospective residents and their families, this information can feel overwhelming and isolating.

Generic sales pitches and resource packets do not address each prospect's unique situation. A more tailored approach, incorporating direct introductions to helpful services, could make a world of difference. A prospect may leave a tour with unanswered questions, and if sales teams do not follow up meaningfully, those concerns remain unresolved. Many communities fail to nurture prospects through ongoing engagement, allowing uncertainty and fear to linger.

The most successful communities recognize that their role is not just to provide information but to actively partner with, engage, and guide prospects through the transition process. By simplifying the journey, they create a supportive experience that builds trust and reduces hesitation. Rather than overwhelming prospects with data, sales teams can offer step-by-step assistance. This may include helping them connect with downsizing experts, financial advisors, or even current residents who can share personal experiences. Be curious and go deeper with your discovery.

It is imperative that you provide a roadmap that breaks down the transition into manageable steps that can make the process feel less intimidating. They need to know that you understand their barriers and have a solution that will guide them along the way. Remember, their timeline may not be visible, but it exists. It's shaped by external pressures: a lease ending, surgery recovery, a spouse's declining health. If the sales process isn't aligned with these realities, opportunities are missed. Pushing for a deposit too soon—or waiting too long—can cost trust and credibility.

Finally, don't assume that an enthusiastic reaction to your tour guarantees that a prospect will move forward. I have had the experience of being in their homes after touring certain communities. As a trusted partner, I get the inside scoop on the real story. A "nice tour!" does not mean "I'm ready to buy." Many teams interpret friendliness or engagement as buying signals, when they may simply reflect politeness or curiosity. Without deep discovery and emotional insight, the pipeline is filled with people who aren't truly moving forward.

5

THE HOLISTIC APPROACH TO SALES

Did you know that communities with integrated move-in support services see 20-30 percent faster conversion rates compared to those without?

I have always been a natural problem solver and a connector of people, driven by a passion for providing resources that empower others. It's my superpower! Being from a family of educators (my mother is a retired teacher and both my sisters are also educators), it's no surprise that my career path has been rooted in teaching and mentorship. After college, I chose to work within the adult education system, helping high school dropouts and teen mothers navigate their way to success. I then began teaching in the Human Services field in higher education. In my case management and crisis intervention courses, one of the most important lessons I taught my students was that having information and resources isn't enough; it's only useful if you know how to apply it. Resources without context are just data points on a list. People in need don't just require information; they need guidance from someone who understands their challenges and is willing to walk the journey with them. As part of a course project, my students were tasked with creating a resource notebook. This wasn't just about compiling a list of services but required them to deeply understand each resource, including the services provided, fees, hours of operation, and accessibility. To ensure accuracy, I would spot-check their work by directly contacting the organizations in their notebooks.

Through this exercise, my students learned a critical lesson: when someone is in need or facing a crisis, the last thing they want is to be handed a list of phone numbers and left to figure it out alone. Instead, they need informed guidance, practical support, and a clear path forward. The time and effort invested in curating the right resources made a tangible difference, proving to be an invaluable tool in truly supporting those they served.

The Holistic Approach

When you move to a new town, neighborhood, or city what's the first thing you do? You ask for recommendations: a good school, a reliable lawn care service, or a trustworthy housekeeper. You don't want to spend hours researching and making calls, trying to determine who is reputable and who isn't. A warm introduction from someone who has firsthand experience with a service provider saves time, reduces stress, and eliminates uncertainty. Starting from scratch can be overwhelming as you may not even know what questions to ask, what fair pricing looks like, or what regulations you need to consider.

What if communities took the same approach when assisting prospects—Instead of simply handing out vendor lists filled with movers, real estate agents, and downsizing specialists? They are taking an active role in guiding residents through the process. While these lists are well-intentioned, they often create more confusion than clarity, leaving prospects with an overwhelming number of options and no clear starting point. Too many choices can lead to decision fatigue and hesitation. What your customers need isn't just a list; they need trusted recommendations, personal connections, and reassurance from professionals who can help them navigate this major transition with confidence.

When I visited clients in their homes for consultations, I had the privilege of entering into their most vulnerable and safe spaces. I waited for them to offer me a seat, which was normally at their kitchen or dining room table. As I sat with them, I often saw several information packets from prior community tours. Additionally, there would be a stack of brochures and business cards with various recommendations like organizers, realtors, estate planners, auctioneers, and moving companies. Each community packet also included referrals along with multiple apartment floor plan options. I would ask them questions about their options, and they would share that they would rather just stay in their homes and didn't really need to move right now. I could see the defeat in their eyes and voice. Even as a professional in this space, it was difficult for me to help them navigate through it all. Where do they even begin? What questions do they ask? Who can they trust?

A holistic approach to sales means looking beyond simply providing a product or service. It involves truly understanding a prospect's challenges, concerns, and emotional needs. Similar to wraparound services used in counseling, active adult and senior living sales teams need to act as guides and advocates for their prospects, offering comprehensive support throughout the transition process. The goal is to provide solutions that address every part of the journey through a person-centered approach.

A full-circle experience means ensuring that every touchpoint in the sales process contributes to a seamless transition. It's about making prospects feel supported from the initial inquiry to move-in day and beyond. By staying proactive, communities can eliminate stressors before they become obstacles. Ensuring follow-ups, check-ins, and ongoing communication can provide reassurance.

I often hear sales teams say, *"We have to provide multiple resources due to liability concerns. We want to give prospects options to choose from."* While I understand the reasoning behind offering more than one choice, the liability argument raises some important questions. Many communities make exclusive selections when it comes to third-party home care agencies, rehabilitation services, in-house medical providers, salons, and food service vendors. If communities are confident in making these suggestions in critical areas, shouldn't the same level of discernment be applied when recommending move management, real estate, or downsizing services? Of course, a proper vetting process must be in place, but it is the same concept.

Instead of simply providing a list of various resources, try actively facilitating introductions between prospects and service providers. This creates a sense of trust and makes the transition smoother. You can arrange calls or in-person meetings between prospects and vetted vendors. Working with trusted professionals who have experience with senior transitions can make a significant difference. By facilitating personal introductions and offering direct support, you can build trust and ultimately accelerate the decision-making process.

Here are a few ideas for connecting a prospect with a vendor right After the Tour:

In-Person or Three-Way Phone/Virtual Introduction:

"Hi, Mrs. Thompson, I'd love for you to speak with someone I trust who's helped many of our residents through this exact transition. This is Sarah, a move management specialist who can walk you through the next steps—from planning your move to settling in comfortably. She's truly wonderful at making things feel less overwhelming. Also, as a reminder, we will be paying up to $$$ towards your floor planning and move management services."

Email or Written Introduction:

Subject: A Helpful Introduction for Your Transition

Hi Mr. Davis,

As we discussed during your visit, many of our residents have found support through trusted professionals during their move. I'd like to introduce you to Mark from [*Vendor*

Company Name], who specializes in helping people just like you manage downsizing and moving logistics. He's familiar with our community and can provide guidance tailored to your needs.

Feel free to reach out to him directly, or let me know if you'd like me to set up a time for you both to talk. Also, don't forget that we will be paying up to $$$ towards your floor planning and move management services.

Warmly,
The Perfect Salesperson

In-Person or Three-Way Phone/Zoom Introduction (Estate Sale/Auction Vendor)

"Mr. Reynolds, one of the things that can feel overwhelming is figuring out what to do with a lifetime of belongings. That's why I want to introduce you to Diane. She runs a trusted estate sales and auction company we've worked with many times. She's fantastic at helping people sort, organize, and find value in their items, with dignity and care. I think she'll be a great resource for you as you plan your next steps."

They Don't Know What They Don't Know

Most clients are not fully aware of what they need. Effective discovery means asking the right questions and truly listening for clues to identify their underlying concerns and priorities.

- Understanding the "Why" Behind the Move: Many struggle to articulate what's driving their decision, and guiding them through this reflection can help accelerate their journey.

- Addressing Unspoken Fears: Prospects hesitate due to underlying concerns they haven't voiced, such as fear of losing independence, social isolation, or financial worries.

Taking a holistic approach to sales means being more than just a salesperson; it means being an advocate, a guide, and a trusted advisor. By providing wraparound services, creating a seamless experience, and uncovering hidden needs, sales teams can build deeper relationships with prospects, making their transition smoother and more confident. This proactive, empathetic approach ultimately leads to higher satisfaction and stronger community engagement (Holleran, 2024).

Examples include:

- Creating time for a home visit, or leveraging your trusted provider on your behalf.
- Setting a realistic timeline for downsizing and moving.
- Connecting prospects with real estate professionals who specialize in active adult and senior moves.
- Offering planning workshops or seminars to address common concerns.

  "They gave me a checklist that made everything feel doable. It turned my anxiety into action." – George, eighty, prospective resident.

Following up with prospects isn't just about checking in but about continuing the conversation in a meaningful and supportive way. Too often, follow-ups feel transactional rather than personal, which can make prospects feel like just another name on a list or a task in your CRM. Successful follow-ups are intentional, timely, and personalized to the individual's concerns and interests.

Instead of generic emails or sales pitches, follow-ups can be based on previous conversations and specific concerns. Prospects often have lingering questions after a tour, and addressing those in follow-ups can alleviate concerns and move them closer to a decision. Following up too soon can feel pushy, while waiting too long can lead to lost interest. Finding the right balance is key.

> *"I wasn't expecting them to remember our conversation about my dog, but when they followed up and mentioned how pet-friendly the community was, it made me feel like they truly cared." – Nancy, seventy-four, prospective resident.*

Genuine relationships aren't built overnight, but they are essential in guiding prospects toward informed and confident decisions. By practicing attentive follow-up, prioritizing listening, and fostering trust, sales teams can create meaningful connections that not only help fill communities but also ensure long-term satisfaction among residents. When prospects feel heard, supported, and valued, they are more likely to move forward with confidence, knowing they are making the right choice.

6
HAVING IT THEIR WAY

*If you go to a fast-food place and they tell you
exactly what to eat, you might walk away, but if
they let you build your perfect meal, you feel like
you're in control. They will be intentional in learning more about what you like, whether you have
allergies, and your budget. The same works for your
prospects. Give them choices, guide them, but let
them feel empowered in their decision.*

The famous slogan, *"Have It Your Way,"* transformed the
fast-food industry by giving customers control over
their meals. I read an article that Burger King launched
a contest offering customers the chance to win a million
dollars for their ultimate Whopper creation. The question was simple: *"How would you top your Whopper?"* It
asked customers to be creative in imagining their dream
Whopper. Although they've already offered more than
two-hundred thousand customizations since their incep-
tion in 1957, they wanted to provide customers with the

opportunity to experience and share their own ideas (February, 2004).

This same principle can be applied to your sales approach: your prospects want a personalized experience tailored to their unique needs, preferences, and concerns, rather than being forced into a one-size-fits-all model. How freeing it is to have choices! Just as customers appreciate customizing their meals, prospective residents want to feel that they are making the decisions that best fit their lifestyle. Offering various move-in plans, different levels of care, and customizable living arrangements can make your future residents feel more in control of their journey.

I can't count the number of sales staff that I have met and toured with. Sometimes I think I could lead a tour in my sleep. As a business partner, I listen for opportunities to engage with them on their needs. For instance, when they took me to the model apartment, it was the perfect opportunity for me to inquire about who takes care of their model moves, or who decorates them. Most of them would say their maintenance staff does it all. Truth be told, your maintenance staff strongly dislikes breaking down, moving, and setting up your model apartments. How do I know? They've told me. Most of them are overworked and have a list of other priorities that are necessary to maintain the community. I am sure their time could be better spent elsewhere than making beds and hanging artwork in a model apartment.

Communities follow a standard sales script, offering the same tour experience, the same information packets, and the same pricing structures to every prospect.

However, just as no two prospects are alike, no two sales experiences should be identical. If I can anticipate your tour patterns and talk tracks, so can your prospects. Stop feature dumping and providing them with information they don't want or need. Instead, ask them what they want to see. Ask them what they want to know that will help them feel at ease with the process. If they're not an artist, why are you showing them the art room? Also, remember that this may not be the only community they tour. If it all begins to sound the same, they will most likely tune out.

Tailoring their experience can help them get their needs met. Some prospects are looking for immediate medical support, while others are seeking a vibrant social environment. Understanding their priorities allows for a customized approach. Instead of overwhelming prospects with a one-size-fits-all tour, intentional sales teams take the time to understand specific concerns and create a plan that directly addresses them. If they're an avid reader and book club enthusiast, bypass the beauty parlor and take them straight to the library.

A personalized sales journey, tailored to each prospect's needs, also ensures that they will feel valued and understood rather than just handled, like any other potential customer. A customized approach starts with building rapport and trust with the prospect. Whether it's letting prospects choose how they receive information (in person, via email, or through video calls) or allowing them to engage with the community at their own pace, giving them options makes them feel more comfortable. Instead of generic follow-up calls, touching base about specific concerns or interests they shared on the tour makes a lasting impression.

I believe the best sales strategies mirror the concept behind *"Have It Your Way"* by offering a highly personalized and flexible experience. Prospects want to feel empowered in their decisions, and communities that tailor their approach to each individual will stand out. Avoiding cookie-cutter solutions, while actively listening and crafting a tailored journey leads to stronger connections, greater trust, and ultimately, more confident move-ins.

7
WHAT IS YOUR COMMUNITY READINESS IQ?

Your teams are selling to more than just your prospects. They are also selling to their preferred partnerships. We are the ones who are in the community talking about you, your community, and your readiness IQ. Be sure your teams are genuine and brand well. Your community's readiness IQ assessment doesn't just measure metrics; it reveals the operational and human readiness of your team to succeed in today's senior living and fifty-five+ housing market. Your metrics alone aren't enough. Your team's talent, mindset, and execution style are equally important in determining long-term sales success. This is important, as it is costing you time and resources.

I recently asked a top-performing salesperson from an active adult community what she believed made her so successful. In her usual humble tone, she simply said, *"I'm intentional—I'm not salesy."* She explained that by the time a buyer walks in for a tour, they're not just browsing out of curiosity. They've been researching, talking with family, and seriously thinking about what this next chapter might look like.

She focuses on connection first: building genuine rapport. Then, early in the conversation, she asks a bold but honest question: *"Are you ready to make a decision to move?"* At first, I was surprised by her directness. I'm used to sales teams slowly working prospects through objections and trying to build momentum. But her approach is refreshingly different. She meets people where they are and respects their readiness without pressure.

Depending on how the prospect responds, she takes one of two routes: If they're serious, she helps them move forward in finding their new home. If they're still unsure, she adds them to a follow-up list and keeps them engaged with event updates and special offers—no pressure, just presence.

I asked if her confidence came from experience and tenure, assuming most new salespeople wouldn't feel comfortable being so candid. Her answer stuck with me. She said it's not just about years in the role; it's about focus and time management. She's confident in the product she represents and in the process she's guiding people through. She deeply values the relationship she builds with each prospect and understands that her time—and theirs—is valuable.

Being a top performer, she explained, means knowing when to move forward and when to pause. And that clarity, rooted in respect and honesty, is what makes her stand out.

Characteristics of High-Performing Sales Professionals:

- **Empathy**: Top closers understand the emotional weight prospects carry. They listen with compassion and tailor their guidance accordingly.

- **Curiosity**: They ask thoughtful, open-ended questions and probe beyond surface objections. Remember, they showed up to tour for a reason.

- **Consultative Mindset**: They don't push; they solve. They view themselves as guides, not just salespeople.

- **Confidence with Complexity**: They are comfortable navigating complicated timelines, family dynamics, or logistical barriers.

- **Follow-Through**: Great sales professionals don't just make contact; they build trust over time through consistent, value-driven follow-up.

Red Flags to Watch For:

- Over-reliance on scripts or price-based selling
- Not believing in your company or product
- Avoiding conversations about logistics or transitions
- Missing emotional cues from prospects or families
- Using the same approach with every prospect, regardless of need
- Only focusing on the number of move-ins you need to meet your goals or receive your bonus

Is Your Team Set Up to Win?

- Are your leaders training sales teams on both emotional AND logistical discovery?

- Are you giving your sales team permission (and time) to build relationships instead of just closing transactions?

- Have you invested in preferred partnerships that support the entire transition, not just the tour?

- Do you allow your teams to go deeper in exploration through home visits, partnership introductions, and program offerings that work?

When you focus on human readiness and strategic support, the result is a confident, equipped sales team that closes faster, builds better relationships, and becomes a trusted resource in the community.

Invest in Your People

What's your community's readiness IQ? And how are you investing in your people to improve it?

Improving readiness is not just about refining your processes; it's about cultivating the talent and confidence of the people who bring your community's vision to life. One of the most effective ways to elevate your readiness IQ is by investing in your team's development in a meaningful and sustainable way. Well-trained teams can better respond to the needs of your prospects, enhancing their overall experience, retention, and satisfaction.

This starts with providing training that goes beyond scripts. Sales professionals need real-time guidance on how to navigate emotional and logistical conversations with care and confidence. Workshops that focus on full discovery—uncovering not just what prospects want, but what's holding them back—can lead to more effective, customized sales approaches. The team at KD Consulting Group offers half-day, full-day and weekend intensives just for this purpose. Mentorship and shadowing programs offer an opportunity for team members to observe and learn from experienced closers in real time. These moments are often where salespeople gain the practical, nuanced skills that can't be taught in manuals.

Equipping teams with vetted toolkits of trusted transition partners also lowers insecurities and strengthens their confidence. Instead of handing out generic vendor lists, your salespeople can offer direct introductions to professionals they know and trust, turning uncertainty into action for your prospects. Yes, this takes time and investment, but helping your prospects transition comfortably and with ease is worth it.

Recognition is another key. Don't just celebrate move-ins but acknowledge the behaviors that lead to them. Documented discovery notes, well-facilitated vendor connections, and thoughtful problem-solving are all signs of a high-readiness sales culture. What sets your sales teams apart? Finally, prioritize confidence-building over compliance. Practice having hard conversations, such as discussing affordability, family dynamics, or fears about moving. When your team is prepared for these moments with full answers and solutions, they can guide prospects through them with empathy and professionalism. Remember, this is not a population that walks into a potential new home for the first time and signs a lease on the spot.

My background in professional counseling has been a gift in this work. I had the privilege of being trained in family dynamics, interviewing techniques, crisis intervention, and group facilitation—skills that directly translate into understanding and supporting people during major life transitions. I recognize that not every salesperson or sales training program includes this kind of foundation. But in today's senior living and active adult landscape, it should.

Investing in the right training is not optional; it's essential to the success of your community. The most valuable investment you can make is in people who know how to move others forward, not just logistically but also emotionally. True readiness isn't just about strategy or scripts; it's a combination of insight, empathy, and consistency. When your team embodies that, everything else falls into place.

What is Your Community Readiness IQ?

Is your sales team prepared to support prospects through a full transition process? Use KD Consulting's assessment to evaluate whether your sales team and community are fully leveraging transition services to drive conversions, reduce costs, and increase occupancy.

Section 1: Sales Cycle & Conversion:

1. Is your average sales cycle longer than ninety days?
2. Do less than 25 percent of tours result in move-ins?
3. Are you struggling to retain priority list prospects over six+ months?

4. Have you lost move-ins due to delays related to downsizing or home sales?

Section 2: Logistical Support Integration

5. Do you only provide a vendor list without personal introductions or guided referrals?

6. Are your sales team members uncomfortable or unsure how to address the logistics of moving with prospects?

7. Have you received feedback from prospects or adult children about being overwhelmed by the moving process?

Section 3: Marketing & Financial ROI

8. Is your cost per move-in exceeding $10,000?

9. Are you offering incentives that don't directly address the prospect's barriers to moving forward?

10. Has your team struggled to show ROI from marketing efforts or promotions?

Section 4: Community Differentiation

11. Does your messaging primarily focus on amenities and pricing, rather than solving real-world transition barriers?

12. Do competitors offer more robust relocation, downsizing, or move-in support than your community?

Scoring:

- **0–3 Yes Answers**: Your team is aligned with best practices—look for advanced support strategies to maintain your edge.

- **4–7 Yes Answers**: There are key opportunities to reduce friction in your sales process and better support prospects. You would benefit from targeted training, vendor integration, and logistical incentives.

- **8+ Yes Answers**: Your sales team and marketing investments may be underperforming. You need a comprehensive partnership to transform your conversion pipeline.

What This Means:

If you answered "yes" to several questions, your team may be leaving valuable move-ins on the table.

PART THREE

CROSSING THE BRIDGE

8
LEAN ALL THE WAY IN

"I used to wait until the last minute to introduce moving services. Now, we bring them in during the first visit. Prospects see the full picture and feel more prepared. Move-in times have gone from months to weeks. Once they know help is available, they're ready to commit sooner."

— Director of Sales, CCRC

Only 14 percent of sales teams actively incorporate third-party partnerships into their process, yet those who do report higher prospect confidence and faster move-ins (Salesforce, 2022).

Over the past decade, I've interviewed several sales counselors in both the active adult and senior living communities, always eager to learn about their processes, challenges, and the changes they wish to see. One key question I always ask is: *At what point in the sales process do you begin discussing logistics with the client?* It's evident that many prospects are proactively thinking about downsizing and logistical challenges *before* touring communities.

Recognizing and addressing these concerns early in the engagement process can enhance trust and facilitate smoother transitions for potential residents.

The responses vary depending on the type of community, but most sales teams hesitate to address the "how" until a financial commitment is made, fearing it might overwhelm the prospect. This delayed approach has always puzzled me. The reality is that prospects have been thinking about the "how" long before they even step into a sales office. Many have already had discussions with their families about the "how," "why," and "when" of their move. Instead of avoiding these conversations, why not anticipate their concerns and guide them through the process from the start?

Research and industry insights indicate that many prospects begin considering downsizing and logistical planning well before scheduling a tour. Consumers are cost-conscious about every aspect of their lives. In fact, financial affordability ranks as the number one concern.

A survey conducted by myLifeSite revealed that the process of downsizing and preparing to sell one's current home is often perceived as a significant obstacle to moving into a retirement community. Respondents highlighted concerns about the logistics of downsizing, indicating that these considerations are top-of-mind even before engaging with specific communities.

One of the most effective ways to speed up the decision-making process is by embedding supportive services into the sales journey from the very beginning. Prospects often delay their decisions because they feel overwhelmed by the logistics of moving, financial concerns, or emotional attachments to their current home. By addressing these challenges upfront, communities can help eliminate barriers and make the transition smoother.

Transparency with support yields success. Lean all the way in by anticipating these concerns, rather than waiting for prospects to express financial concerns. Sales teams can proactively offer resources, such as consultations with financial planners or home sale assistance. Instead of a generic approach, tailoring services to each prospect's unique needs can accelerate their decision-making timeline. Have you ever tried adding your logistical support information to your website and collateral? What about listing it right under the home sale price? Why not let your prospects know from the very beginning that you have their back?

Dedication of Time and Resources

I'll admit that building a truly successful process requires a significant investment of time and resources. As I mentioned earlier, I've spent countless hours meeting with various sales teams, touring for-profit and not-for-profit communities, and engaging in events. I have deep respect for their tenacity, professionalism, and dedication to each prospect. Adding yet another task to their already full plates can feel overwhelming. The real question is: *How important is it for an operator to invest in a holistic program that bridges the gaps to occupancy?*

Strong partnerships with trusted service providers can significantly reduce the stress associated with moving into a community. Sales teams can actively build and maintain relationships with real estate agents, moving companies, senior transition experts, and other relevant service providers. By introducing supportive partners to anticipate their concerns, you can more effectively guide them through the entire process. They will have more confidence in you, the trusted expert, and your community as a result. Confidence is necessary in order to build trust. And without trust, there is no sale.

If you aren't meeting the needs of your prospects, can you be more impactful and effective in closing the deal? I often wonder if the financial cost of a prospect's transition should be discussed alongside the financial commitment of their unit. Many community information packets outline costs for various plans, monthly services, and medical expenses, yet rarely include an estimate of what it might actually cost to make the move. When I've provided cost estimates for clients, most weren't interested in every individual line item; they wanted to know the total, all-in cost so they could plan accordingly. Clients don't want unexpected add-ons or surprise fees; they want a clear understanding of what to expect. While I understand the hesitation in presenting large numbers upfront, offering a transparent cost roadmap could provide much-needed clarity and ease in making one of the biggest decisions of their lives. Collaborate with your providers and give prospects a ballpark figure.

While it's important to accelerate the decision process, trust should never be sacrificed. Your prospects need to feel confident that they are making the right choice. Building trust through transparency, education, and continuous support can help shorten the sales cycle. Providing clear, honest information upfront prevents delays caused by unanswered questions or misconceptions. Assigning a dedicated point of contact to guide prospects through the process will make all the difference. Accelerating the decision cycle isn't about pressuring prospects; it's about removing obstacles, providing solutions, and building trust. By embedding supportive services early, forming strong partnerships, and maintaining a personalized, transparent approach, you can help prospects feel confident and ready to make their move. A smooth, well-supported transition leads to happier residents and stronger communities.

It's Not About The Money

Consider how your community's messaging and branding align with the experience you provide. What impact will this process have on your reputation? Picture the conversations happening at their kitchen table as they weigh their options between two or three communities. What sets yours apart? Why would they choose you over the others? More importantly, what will they tell their friends and family about their experience with your process? I remember meeting with an executive director for a CCRC to discuss the value of creating a built-in program that actively helps reservists move forward in the process. Many communities offer occasional incentives like reducing the monthly rent, waiving community fees, or offering discounts on finishes and upgrades. While these are appealing, they don't actually assist prospects in making the transition; they only benefit them after they've moved in. I suggested a different approach: providing direct support for their move by covering a portion of the costs. I shared several ways this program could be structured, and I presented her with a plan. In response, she asked, *"Kiera, these people are wealthy. Why would I give them money toward their move?"* Unfortunately, this wasn't the first time I had heard a sentiment like this. Others have expressed concerns about budget constraints, the impact on their department's finances, or the challenge of determining who should receive the incentive.

Here's the reality: It is not about the money. Whether a person is wealthy or poor, healthy or unhealthy, young or old, moving is still the third most stressful event in a person's life. By offering them an incentive, you ease that stress, no matter how wealthy they are. By customizing and designing a road map for your prospects that includes a proven solution to help with their logistical needs, your brand and messaging will radiate as, *"We understand your barriers and we are here to support your journey from beginning to end. We will help you however we can."*

To effectively support the growing aging population, both the senior living and move management industries must evolve by providing comprehensive, end-to-end support. This includes integrating moving services, real estate partnerships, and downsizing specialists to ease the transition for residents and their families. Greater outreach and education efforts are needed to raise awareness about available resources, from financial planning to decluttering assistance. Stronger collaboration and team support between senior living communities, real estate professionals, move managers, and financial advisors is essential to creating a seamless experience for seniors. Additionally, staff training goes beyond sales and care to include guidance on moving logistics, home sales, and lifestyle adjustments. Recognizing that every senior has unique needs, the industry must also offer personalized solutions such as staggered move-ins, rental options, or trial stays to facilitate a smoother transition.

EXAMPLE ROAD MAP

Your Journey, Simplified: A Step-by-Step Roadmap to Your New Home

- **Discovery & Personal Planning**
  - **Sample Language You Can Use:** *"Let's understand your goals."*
  - We will begin with you. Meet with a sales advisor to discuss lifestyle desires, health needs, family input, and emotional concerns. Tailor the roadmap based on the individual's journey.
  - Explain the full process of the roadmap, leaving room for them to add other needs, e.g., medical, pharmaceutical, financial planning, etc.

- **Downsizing & Home Prep Consultation**
  - **Sample Language You Can Use:** *"It's not about losing things; it's about keeping what matters."*
  - Personally introduce them to one of your vetted specialists or move managers to begin creating a customized project plan. This may include floor planning to understand what will fit into their new home, organizing, or preparing the current home for sale.
  - If your client is an art collector or has antiques, you will need to connect them with your high-end art dealer or estate sales professional.

- **Real Estate Guidance**
  - **Sample Language You Can Use:** *"Selling your home, simplified."*
  - Introduce them to your trusted real estate partner to assess market value, timing, and staging. Coordinate showings and paperwork with minimal stress.
  - Customize the selection of your real estate partners based on your prospect's needs, such as luxury, demographics, knowledge, sales success, and SRES designee.

- **Financial Clarity Session**
  - **Sample Language You Can Use:** *"No financial surprises."*
  - Review all financial aspects of their selection, move, including estimated moving costs, community fees, home sale timing, and alignment with personal goals.
  - You will gain a better knowledge of these based on your relationship with your vetted partners.

- **Move Management Support**
  - **Sample Language You Can Use:** *"Logistics handled."*
  - The selected partner will assist with packing, scheduling movers, coordinating deliveries, and setting up the new space to ensure a seamless transition.

○ Support and mitigate any mishaps. Remember, some of these customers haven't moved in decades. Some have old and fragile furniture.

- **Transition Check-Ins**
  - **Sample Language You Can Use:** *"We're still here."*

  ○ Conduct regular check-ins with both your prospect and partner before and after the move to ensure everything is on track and the individual is adjusting well to the new home and community.

- Welcome Experience
  - **Sample Language You Can Use:** *"You're not just moving in; you're joining us."*

  ○ On move-in day, greet the new resident with a personalized welcome, introduce them to neighbors, and help them feel settled from the start.

9
FOLLOW THE L.E.A.D.ER

Following your leads is more than a follow-up phone call or email. Learning to follow your leads means being their guide throughout their entire process, understanding that you are now committed, invested, and connected with them from the beginning to the end.

I developed the comprehensive **L.E.A.D.er** model (*listen, engage, adapt, deliver, and execute revenue*) to equip sales leaders and operators with a framework that not only helps them actively listen for logistical cues and engage meaningfully with prospects, but also supports operations in building systems that provide real solutions—ensuring prospects have a clear and supported path to actually getting there. Sales training in the active adult and senior living industries has long been built on established methodologies, but not all training programs address the nuances of full discovery from the prospect's perspective. The L.E.A.D.er model is not about replacing existing sales frameworks but rather assessing where improvements can be made and integrating a more consultative, discovery-driven process. By embedding this approach into current systems, sales teams can better align with the emotional and logistical needs of prospective residents and their families. I want sales professionals to learn more about the barriers to entry and develop the skills to uncover information that may not otherwise be shared.

The **L.E.A.D.er** model is designed to guide sales teams in creating deeper connections and uncovering the full scope of a prospect's needs. Each step represents a crucial phase of the sales journey. As the industry changes, we must be willing to assess and audit our current processes.

Why the L.E.A.D.er Model?

- Helps teams listen for key logistical cues
- Encourages meaningful engagement with prospects
- Aligns sales and operations around the client journey
- Builds systems that provide real solutions
- Supports prospects in confidently getting there

Examples of the L.E.A.D.er Model in Action:

L – **Listen** – Understand what your prospect isn't saying.

Actionable Step: Practice active, empathetic, and active listening during every interaction. Ask open-ended questions that go beyond surface needs. Listen for cues of logistical barriers to entry.

Language you can use:

- During a tour, ask: *"What's been the hardest part of thinking about this move?" "What's holding you back from making a decision?"*

- Take note of emotional triggers and cues (e.g., fear of leaving a longtime home, loss of independence, family pressure).

- Allowing strangers into their homes.

- Repeat back what you hear: *"It sounds like you're concerned about downsizing too much. Let's explore options that feel comfortable."*

E – Engage

Actionable Step: Build trust by making personal, meaningful connections. Show you're an advocate, not just a salesperson.

Implementation Example:

- Personally introduce them to one of your preferred partners (e.g., move manager, real estate agent, estate sales) who can walk them through the next steps.

- Send a handwritten card After the Tour referencing a shared moment (e.g., *"I loved hearing about your garden on Maple Street. Our community courtyard might be a perfect next chapter."*)

- Host small "Coffee & Conversation" or "Wine Down" gatherings for prospects to meet current residents.

A – Adapt – Meet prospects where they are, not where you want them to be.

Actionable Step: Customize your communication and solutions to match each prospect's situation—emotionally, culturally, and logistically.

Implementation Example:

- Offer a weekday afternoon visit for a prospect who doesn't drive at night.
- Schedule a virtual call.
- Present two floor plans with personalization options (if possible, use their furniture measurements. This is the perfect time to implement your preferred partner to design their floor plans).
- If a prospect is uncomfortable discussing finances openly, introduce a neutral third-party resource for financial planning or bridge loan options.
- Offer to 'test drive" the experience with overnight stays.
- Accommodate their hesitation needs (floor plan, downsize, etc.)

D – Deliver – Show consistency, reliability, and progress.

Actionable Step: Follow through on every commitment and create micro-wins that build trust and momentum.

Implementation Example:

- If you promised a virtual tour for their daughter, schedule it within twenty-four hours.
- Keep a shared "move prep timeline" with check-ins every week (e.g., *"Have you contacted your move manager yet? Here's what to expect next."*). Design the roadmap together and use it as an actionable guide.
- Provide a "Welcome Home Plan" that outlines everything from utility transfers to first-week

activities after move-in. I recommend presenting them with the full plan, then working on it in phases to reduce the overwhelming pressures.

er – Execute Revenue – Drive successful outcomes through value, not pressure.

Actionable Step: Drive conversion by connecting the emotional and logistical solutions to the sale. Create urgency through readiness and relationship. Be the bridge and take ownership. People buy from people and systems they trust.

Implementation Example:

- Say: *"You've already connected with our move team and reserved a floor plan that fits your needs. Let's set a move-in date so we can help you transition on your terms."*
- Design a value-based program (e.g., free floor planning consultation, downsizing, and unpacking support) tied to deposit deadlines. *"After your deposit, you will receive XXX service from us!"*
- Convert trust and logistics into committed next steps.
- Simply put, provide the service support that will close the deal.
- Track each prospect's sales journey with status updates and team accountability (sales + operations). Leverage your preferred partners.

As the industry evolves, we must continually assess, reassess, audit, and adapt our processes to meet the needs and concerns of our prospects. We must keep the focus on them. Traditional sales training often emphasizes presenting features and benefits, but prospects are not just looking for a community; they are navigating a life transition. Sales teams that fail to conduct a full discovery risk missing critical insights that could mean the difference between hesitation and commitment. It's also important to note that the adult children will thank you later.

A thorough discovery process involves understanding the emotional motivations behind a move, such as family encouragement, health changes, or lifestyle improvements. It also requires identifying logistical barriers, such as home sales, downsizing, financial concerns, or hesitancy to leave familiar surroundings. Additionally, assessing the decision-making timeline and key influencers helps uncover hidden objections that prospects may not immediately express. By prioritizing discovery, sales professionals can tailor their approach, address concerns proactively, and offer solutions that align with each prospect's unique journey.

Implementing The L.E.A.D.er Model

Rather than overhauling an organization's sales training, my **L.E.A.D.er** method is designed to enhance what is already in place. I work with sales teams to take a deep dive into their current processes, while integrating solutions from the client's perspective. We assess their current training by evaluating the sales process, journey mapping, and assessing whether it prioritizes active listening over simply presenting information. It's important to align with the prospect's timeline rather than focusing solely on sales goals. Successful sales professionals have the tools to adapt conversations based on discovery, offering personalized solutions instead of just general community details. Additionally, addressing emotional barriers and decision hesitations is crucial to guiding prospects through the transition with confidence and support.

By identifying gaps, communities can implement the **L.E.A.D.er** model to strengthen their existing approach and improve conversion rates. For organizations seeking to enhance their sales approach, the **L.E.A.D.er** model provides supplementary training modules that enhance sales professionals' skills. These include *Advanced Discovery Training*, which helps uncover true motivators and concerns beyond surface-level questions; *Emotional Intelligence in Sales*, which focuses on understanding decision-making psychology and building trust through genuine connections; *Logistical Navigation*, which equips teams with holistic expertise in move management, downsizing support, and financial options for a full-service experience; and *Closing with Confidence*, which leverages discovery insights to create a seamless and natural transition toward commitment.

By integrating this model, sales and operations teams can move beyond transactional conversations and instead guide prospects through a personalized, needs-based journey. The result is higher conversion rates, stronger relationships, and a more effective, consultative sales experience for both the community and the prospect.

Creating Built-In Partnerships

I had the opportunity to work with a for-profit rental community designed for adults aged sixty-two+. Before a sales director was even hired, I used my relationship-building skills to connect directly with the builder and position myself as a valuable partner from the ground up. Once the sales director came on board, I was introduced as a trusted resource and quickly began building rapport with her.

Like many blue-sky developments, the community faced the common challenge of engaging and retaining prospects without a sales trailer or model homes to tour. Selling the dream before the first shovel hits the ground isn't easy. That's where I stepped in; not as a vendor, but as a strategic partner. Together, we created marketing and engagement events, often meeting prospects in local coffee shops or restaurants to establish trust and build excitement. I wasn't just another vendor. I was seen as an extension of her team. Because of her limited budget and staff, she welcomed the support.

One major win was getting approval to offer customized floor plans to priority depositors. While refundable deposits always carry financial risk, the greater risk was in losing qualified prospects due to a lack of personalization. That decision helped us retain interest and stand out from the competition.

As construction progressed and a formal sales office opened, we kept building momentum. One of my concierge consultants began working on-site two mornings a week. She'd quietly work in the lobby area, jumping into action whenever a tour wrapped up. The sales director would seamlessly transition prospects to my concierge consultant, who would immediately discuss floor planning, schedule home visits, and outline the move process.

It was seamless and effective—a true one-two punch that elevated the customer experience.

Soon, my concierge consultant became so familiar with the community that she began leading tours herself. She could speak to both the physical space *and* the logistics of moving in. As prospects walked through model units, she would provide real-time advice on furniture fit, repurposing ideas, and tailored move strategies. It brought the dream to life. Before the prospect left the community, she already had a follow-up home visit scheduled for further discovery. It was a tag team collaborative effort.

When unexpected construction delays pushed back the opening date, the sales director called us immediately. Several residents were already en route and needed temporary solutions. We stepped in with quick, flexible support, arranging storage and addressing last-minute logistical issues. The operator was incredibly grateful. Because we had embedded ourselves so thoroughly into the community's process, we could act swiftly and provide peace of mind. Our involvement reduced stress for residents and allowed the sales team to stay focused on closing. This kind of integrated partnership wasn't just helpful, it was transformative and retaining.

Allow me to summarize this strategic plan for you:

Overview:

A new sixty-two+ rental community faced the challenge of collecting deposits and leasing units before the building was complete. Without a sales trailer or models, the sales team needed creative, relationship-driven strategies to engage early prospects and convert them into future residents.

Solution:

By embedding a trusted partner into the early planning and sales process, the community created a high-touch, high-trust environment that kept prospects engaged, even through construction delays.

Timeline & Tactics:

- **Pre-Sales Phase**
  - Developed a relationship with the builder before the sales team was hired.
  - Positioned ourselves as a *business solution* rather than a traditional vendor.
  - Supported the newly hired sales director by co-hosting coffee meetings, events, and informal prospect gatherings.
- **Personalized Incentives**
  - Advocated for and helped implement complimentary custom floor plans for depositors. Prospects put down a $1,000 deposit, and floor plans averaged $300-$500 based on unit size.
  - Helped convert tentative leads into confident future residents.
- **On-Site Integration**
  - Assigned a dedicated concierge to work two mornings a week from the sales office.
  - Provided real-time feedback on furniture fit and move planning after tours.

o Created a seamless "handoff" from tour to move plan and logistical discussion.

o Scheduled follow-up home visits immediately After the Tour.

- **Crisis Support During Delays**

  o The community opening was delayed and we stepped in with emergency storage, move support, and reassurance to residents en route.

  o We maintained momentum and prevented sales fallout.

  o Acted as the mediator and liaison for the sales team.

Outcome:

- The sales team stayed focused on sales while our team reduced logistical stress for incoming residents.

- Our embedded presence elevated trust and created a seamless customer journey.

- The operator expressed deep appreciation for our role in preserving both relationships and revenue.

Key Takeaways:

- **Start early:** Involve trusted logistical and service partners *before* the building opens to build stronger engagement. Build in your messaging.

- **Position partners as extensions of the team:** When prospects see you working as one unit, it creates confidence and reduces friction.

- **Personalize early and often:** Offering things like floor planning upfront—even at a cost—can pay off by improving retention of high-value leads.

- **Be proactive in problem-solving:** When delays hit, embedded partners can step in immediately and save the day.

- **Trust is built in the handoff:** Having a warm introduction from the sales director to the preferred partner keeps momentum and deepens emotional buy-in.

- **Sales teams don't have to do it all:** When logistics, planning, and reassurance are handled by partners, sales leaders can focus on *closing*.

10
BREAKING BARRIERS – REPRESENTATION AND RELATIONSHIPS MATTER

For many prospective residents and their families, deciding to move into a retirement community is already an emotional and logistical challenge. But for individuals from diverse racial, ethnic, or cultural backgrounds, there are additional layers of concern that often go unspoken and unaddressed. Cultural barriers are not only real, they are powerful influences that shape decisions, perceptions, and levels of trust.

For some older adults of color, there is a quiet but deeply felt fear: *Will I be welcomed here? Will I be the only one? Will I feel seen, safe, and understood?* These questions often stem from past experiences with exclusion, microaggressions, or simply a lack of representation. Retirement communities have historically been seen as spaces that primarily serve white, affluent populations. Even when a community is inclusive in practice, the perception may still discourage many from exploring it as an option.

One of the most sensitive yet impactful observations shared by some prospects of color is the discomfort they feel when they tour a community and only see people who look like them working in service roles—housekeeping, dining, or maintenance—rather than in leadership, care, or engagement positions. For many, this dynamic reinforces historical inequities and can be both triggering and discouraging. Representation matters at every level.

Add to that the deeply rooted cultural expectations around aging and caregiving. In many cultures, particularly within African American, Asian, Latino, and immigrant communities, caring for elders is seen as a family responsibility. Turning to a community for support may be viewed as a betrayal of that duty. In some cases, the decision may also be affected by shared financial obligations within extended families, making the cost of care a more complex conversation.

One of the most powerful ways to address these concerns is through representation and storytelling. Prospective residents want to see themselves in the communities they are considering. That means not only showcasing a diverse resident population but also ensuring that staff, from leadership to caregivers, reflect a variety of backgrounds and cultures.

Equally important is hearing from current residents. Real voices and authentic stories from residents who can speak about how they were welcomed, respected, and supported make an enormous difference. These testimonials bridge the gap between perception and reality.

Building Cultural Competency into Community Life

Addressing cultural barriers is not a one-time initiative; it must be baked into the leadership and stakeholders of the community. Warning: Once you make this decision, you must be fully committed to taking initiative and supporting implementation.

This includes:

- Training staff on cultural sensitivity and unconscious bias.
- Offering inclusive programming that celebrates diverse holidays, cuisines, traditions, and languages.
- Hiring and retaining diverse staff at every level.
- Creating affinity groups or culturally relevant support systems that reflect the identities and backgrounds of residents.
- Focusing on the unspoken cues.

To reach communities that have traditionally been underrepresented, operators must expand their outreach strategy. This includes:

- Partnering with cultural organizations, churches, and community leaders who already have trust and influence.
- Participating in multicultural events where education and awareness about senior living options can be shared.
- Developing targeted campaigns that speak to specific concerns and cultural values, using appropriate language, images, and messaging.

There is significant potential for growth among underrepresented groups, particularly within the growing population of African American professionals, Latino retirees, and multigenerational immigrant families. But this potential can only be realized through intentionality, empathy, and cultural fluency.

Communities that are willing to invest in this work will not only expand their reach, but they will also build stronger, more inclusive environments that enhance the quality of life for all residents. There's more to your prospects than what's captured on an intake form. Cultural identity shapes how people view aging, family, independence, and trust. By acknowledging and addressing these realities, not avoiding them, communities can become not just places to live, but places to belong.

Don't Miss the Cues

I recall working with an African American family, primarily the adult daughter, during my time with a move management company. She reached out because of our preferred partnership with a senior living community. When I arrived at her parents' home, her face lit up. Seeing that I, too, was African American brought her visible relief. She embraced me with a warm hug and welcomed me inside, clearly feeling a sense of connection and comfort.

Her father needed assisted living, and her mother, who was experiencing cognitive decline, would soon require memory care. She had already toured the community and was impressed with the services and staff. But as we talked, she asked very intentional questions about how often I'd be at the community, about my relationships with staff, and who would be checking in on her parents. What she really wanted to know, without directly saying it, was whether someone who looked like her parents would be there to ensure they were cared for with dignity and cultural understanding.

This moment revealed a deeper, often unspoken concern—a barrier that could have easily been missed during traditional discovery. While I didn't work for the community, I assured her of my ongoing involvement and shared her concerns with the sales and operational teams. The community responded with sensitivity, making thoughtful adjustments to help the family feel seen and supported.

This experience underscored a powerful truth: prospects often carry concerns they may not voice to your sales or operations teams. Trusted partners can surface these insights and act as bridges—culturally, emotionally, and operationally. If I had shared anything negative about the community, that sale would have been lost. Instead, trust was strengthened, the sale was retained, and the family felt confident moving forward.

Here are some specific tools and recommendations to help you with implementation:

1. Cultural Cues Are Often Unspoken—Train to Recognize Them

Prospects may carry fears they never verbalize—concerns about being seen, accepted, and understood.

Implementation:

- **Sales Training:** Include cultural discovery questions during initial conversations. Incorporate training modules on identifying and responding to cultural cues and emotional undercurrents. Include role-play scenarios where prospects ask indirect questions that signal deeper concerns.

- **Operational Sensitivity:** Teach frontline and leadership staff how subtle cues may indicate a need for cultural representation or concern about inclusion, and how to respond appropriately. Train staff to recognize emotional cues, such as hesitations or hyper-specific questions.

Train sales counselors to ask, "Are there cultural values or expectations you'd like us to understand better as we support your family?"

2. Representation Matters—Visibly and Relationally

Seeing only people of color in service roles can reinforce negative assumptions and deter diverse prospects.

Implementation:

- **Staff Diversity Review:** Conduct a diversity audit of visible staff roles (especially in leadership, caregiving, and sales) to evaluate what prospective residents and families are seeing when they tour. Diversify visible staff in leadership, engagement, and care roles.

- **Intentional Hiring & Mentorship:** Prioritize diverse recruitment and mentorship to ensure leadership tracks reflect the resident population you aim to serve. Reflect authentic diversity in marketing, community events, and onboarding experiences.

- Include photos and stories of diverse staff and residents in brochures, websites, and tours—not just service team members.

   3. **Trusted Partners Provide Crucial Insight—Leverage Them**

Third-party vendors and partners often hear things families won't tell your sales team.

Implementation:

- **Feedback Loops:** Invite preferred vendors, move managers, and referral partners to share common themes or barriers they hear from prospects and families. Get the inside scoop by hosting regular insight meetings to discuss trends, challenges, and feedback from the field. They are your eyes and ears.

- **Partnership Protocols:** Create a system for partners to communicate resident or family concerns to sales and operational teams confidentially and constructively. Create an extension of your teams. Next to your prospects, they are your biggest investment of time, as they can make or break your sales and retention efforts.

- Hold monthly cross-functional meetings that include partners (real estate agents, move managers, etc.) to review soft feedback from the field.

   4. **Emotional Safety Drives Decision Confidence**

Prospects are not just choosing a floor plan; they're choosing peace of mind.

Implementation:

- **Tour Experience Design:** Review your tour and onboarding process. Design the tour experience to feel warm, inclusive, and emotionally responsive. Are there touchpoints where the family feels truly seen and emotionally supported?

- **Welcome Touches:** Assign cultural ambassadors or mentors (staff or resident volunteers) to check in with families from underrepresented groups. Introduce new families to culturally similar staff or resident ambassadors.

After the Tour, follow up with a personalized message from a team member who shares or understands the family's background.

5. Sales Isn't Just About Features; It's About Belonging

It isn't about the amenities; it's about creating a sense of home for your future residents.

Implementation:

- **Discovery Redesign:** Add thoughtful prompts to the discovery process that explore emotional needs, family roles, and past experiences with healthcare, caregiving, or institutions. Shift early-stage conversations toward relational discovery. Lean in and ask the right questions.

- **Language Shift:** Encourage language that prioritizes relationship-building: *"Who will be part of this* *journey with you?"* or *"What does peace of mind look like for your family?"* Use inclusive language that invites participation and shared understanding.

Avoid transactional talk during early conversations. Build emotional context first, then match it with logistical solutions. Ask, "What would a good fit look and feel like for your family?"

Your community's reputation isn't just shaped by the services you offer; it's shaped by the trust you build and the comfort you create. Trusted partners, cultural sensitivity, and representation are not "extras"; they're essentials for converting interest into long-term trust. Sales success is rooted in trust. By acknowledging cultural cues and empowering your partners, you position your community as not just a place to live, but a place where people from all backgrounds and cultures can belong.

Your prospects and families will appreciate it, and they will tell their friends.

When a community can sincerely say, *"We see you. We welcome you. And we're ready to support your unique journey,"* that message becomes a powerful differentiator. It also provides the minority prospect with a sense of security and belonging that will help them realize this is the best community for them.

11
APPLYING IT TO REAL LIFE

"I was skeptical at first, but when we shifted our approach, we saw a 20 percent increase in move-ins. We stopped overwhelming prospects with excessive information and started guiding them through their options—step by step."

— Vanetta, Executive Director.

The best way to illustrate the impact of effective sales strategies is through real-life success stories. Communities that have embraced personalized approaches, proactive guidance, and supportive transition services have seen not only faster move-ins but also higher resident satisfaction. These communities eliminate many of the emotional and logistical hurdles that typically delay a move. By anticipating the needs of prospects and offering tailored solutions, such as individualized transition plans, curated preferred partnerships, and transparent communication, communities build trust more quickly and create a sense of readiness.

For example, rather than offering generic brochures and price lists, successful communities are now designing custom roadmaps for each prospect that outline exactly how their move will be supported, from downsizing and home sale preparation to moving logistics and social integration. Sales teams at these communities are trained to listen deeply, uncover hidden objections, and offer meaningful resources, such as estate sale planning, space planning services, and financial consultations.

The result? Prospects feel seen, heard, and supported. That emotional assurance accelerates their confidence to say "yes" because the unknowns have been proactively addressed. Communities that have embraced personalization and proactive support strategies are witnessing notable improvements in their sales performance metrics, such as shorter sales cycles, increased conversion rates, and stronger word-of-mouth referrals from new residents who describe the move-in process as "surprisingly smooth." By tailoring experiences to individual prospects and addressing logistical concerns upfront, these communities are not only enhancing the decision-making process but also achieving measurable success.

Key Performance Improvements:

- **Conversion Rate Enhancements:** SilverPoint Senior Living reported an inquiry-to-tour conversion rate of 27 percent and a tour-to-move-in rate of 31 percent, surpassing the industry average of 22 percent for inquiry-to-tour conversions.

- **Sales Volume Growth:** Baldwin House Senior Living experienced a 10 to 12 percent increase in sales volume, attributing this growth to personalized offerings and proactive engagement strategies.

These statistics underscore the impact of personalized and proactive approaches in senior living communities, leading to shorter sales cycles, higher conversion rates, and increased resident satisfaction.

Community #1 Non-profit CCRC: This community noticed that many prospects were overwhelmed by the moving process. Instead of simply providing a vendor list, they created an in-house concierge role to personally guide prospects through downsizing, moving logistics, and financial planning. Positive feedback from resident survey results increased by 15 percent.

Community #2 For Profit Rental: Understanding that prospects often struggle with emotional barriers, this community started offering pre-move-in mentorship, where current residents personally connect with potential residents. The sales team noted an uptick in resident referrals with friends.

Community #3 Non-profit Luxury CCRC: Prospects were taking an average of twelve to eighteen months to make a decision. They implemented a comprehensive transition support program, offering moving assistance, financial consultations, and resident mentors. Decision timelines were shortened to six to nine months, and the move-in rate increased by 30 percent.

Community #4 Active Adult Community: Buyers were hesitant due to financial concerns and the stress of their moving logistics and home sale needs. They partnered with professional organizers and realtors to offer one-on-one consultations as part of the sales process. The average time from tour to move-in dropped from fourteen months to seven months.

From these success stories, there are clear takeaways that any active or senior living community can implement to improve their sales process and support prospects more effectively.

- **Create a Transition Concierge Role:** Assign a dedicated staff member, or preferred partner, to help prospects navigate moving logistics, financial concerns, and emotional adjustments. This role is different from a Move-In Coordinator role or an expanded role. This role is client-centered and resource-intensive.

- **Host Peer Mentor Programs:** Pairing prospective residents with current residents helps ease concerns and build confidence in the transition. These interactions can help bridge the gap.

- **Offer "Test Drive" Experiences:** Allow prospects to spend a weekend or a few days in the community before committing. Invite them to pop into the community unannounced to visit and tour.

12
REDEFINING SALES EXCELLENCE

"The future of adult living isn't just about offering a place to live; it's about offering a lifestyle that reflects who we are today, not who we used to be. Communities that recognize our desire for independence, purpose, and ease of transition are the ones that will thrive."

— Karen M., Future Resident
and Active Adult Advocate.

This senior living and active adult industry is evolving rapidly, and sales strategies must keep pace with changing consumer expectations. Today's older adults are more informed, independent, and selective about where they choose to live. They expect more than just a sales pitch; they want a meaningful experience that helps them feel confident about their decision.

- **Move from Selling to Consulting:** Traditional sales tactics that rely on urgency and pressure no longer resonate. The future is rooted in education, support, and guidance.

- **Leverage Technology to Enhance Engagement:** Virtual tours, personalized follow-ups through CRM systems, and digital or virtual engagement strategies help keep prospects connected and informed. Many are already using AI-integrated systems.

- **Adapt to Consumer Preferences:** Today's prospects want choices, flexibility, and a focus on wellness and lifestyle. They're looking to you as the expert to guide.

- **Listen to Understand, Not Just Respond:** Active listening ensures that sales teams truly grasp what prospects want and need.

- **Provide Ongoing Support Beyond the Sale:** Establishing long-term relationships by staying in touch after move-in fosters trust and enhances reputation, and increases retention and word-of-mouth referrals.

- **Tailor Solutions to Individual Needs:** A personalized approach makes all the difference in a prospect's decision-making process.

The best salespeople aren't the ones who talk the most; they're the ones who listen the best. Less pressure, more guidance. Less selling, more comprehensive support. The most successful communities prioritize relationships over transactions. Sales excellence is about creating trust and demonstrating value through a client-centered approach.

That's how you will accelerate decisions and build communities that truly feel like home.

CONCLUSION

Moving the Mission Forward

The decision to move into a new home, especially one meant for the next stage of life, is never simple. It's layered with emotion, timing, trust, finances, and family. And yet, behind every prospect walking through your doors is a deep desire for clarity, confidence, and connection.

Throughout this book, we've explored what holds people back and what propels them forward. We've uncovered the gaps in traditional sales approaches and revealed the power of logistical guidance, warm introductions, emotional intelligence, and community ownership.

If there's one truth I hope you walk away with, it's this: you are not just selling a unit; you are guiding a life transition. And how you show up in those moments matters.

The LEADer model was created for professionals like you. Those who want to lead with intention, listen beyond surface objections, adapt to each unique situation, and deliver not only a beautiful product, but a meaningful experience.

Action Steps: What You Can Do Now

1. **Re-Assess Your Current Process:** Look at your sales touchpoints, tours, and follow-ups. Are you guiding or just informing? Are you solving or just selling?

2. **Integrate Logistical Support Early:** Don't wait until after the deposit. Introduce transition partners, floor planning, and move management resources during discovery.

3. **Train Beyond the Basics:** Invest in your people. Provide sales training that includes emotional readiness, cultural sensitivity, and logistical insight.

4. **Build Relationship Equity:** Follow up with purpose. Personalize every interaction. Become a resource, not just a representative.

5. **Take Ownership:** Your prospects aren't just evaluating the community; they're evaluating whether *you* will walk with them from start to finish. Show them that you will.

This book is not the end; it's your new beginning. A better approach. A more complete solution. And a chance to do the work we were called to do: help people move forward—strategically, thoughtfully, and with heart.

Let's lead them together.

Kiera DesChamps
Founder, KD Consulting Group
Creator of the LEADer Model

SOURCES CITED

CCRC Growth. (2024). *Enhancing Lead Generation Efficiency and Shortening the Sales Cycle for Senior Living Providers Through SEO.* Retrieved from https://ccrgrowth.com/insights/case-studies/enhancing-lead-generation-efficiency-and-shortening-the-sales-cycle-for-senior-living-providers-through-seo/

myLifeSite. (n.d.). *A Predictable Retirement Community Move Holdup.* Retrieved May 14, 2025, from https://mylifesite.net/blog/post/a-predictable-retirement-community-move-holdup/

National Institute on Aging. (2022). *Social Isolation and Loneliness in Older People.* Retrieved from https://www.nia.nih.gov/news/social-isolation-loneliness-older-people-pose-health-risks

National Institute on Aging. (2023). *Advancing Research on Aging Adults.* Retrieved from https://www.nia.nih.gov

National Seniors Australia. (2023). *Downsizing Decisions Among Older Australians.* Retrieved from https://nationalseniors.com.au/uploads/09151399PAC_SeniorsDownsizing_Report_FN_Web.pdf

Pew Research Center. (2022). *Trends in Aging and Retirement Planning.* Retrieved from https://www.pewresearch.org

AARP. (2022). *2022 Home and Community Preferences Survey.* Retrieved from https://www.aarp.org/research/topics/life/info-2022/2022-home-community-preferences.html

Harvard Joint Center for Housing Studies. (2021). *Housing America's Older Adults 2021*. Retrieved from https://www.jchs.harvard.edu/housing-americas-older-adults-2021

Holleran 2024, National Holleran Benchmark. www.holleranconsult.com

National Association of Senior Move Managers (NASMM). (2023). *Industry Trends Report*. Retrieved from https://www.nasmm.org

Salesforce, 2022. State of Sales Report. New research reveals Sales Reps Need a Productivity Overhaul - Spend Less than 30% Of Their Time Actually Selling - Salesforce.

Senior Housing News. (2024, February 12). *Senior Living Operators Level Up Sales to Beat Alarming Trends in Conversions*. Retrieved from https://seniorhousingnews.com/2024/02/12/senior-living-operators-level-up-sales-to-beat-alarming-trends-in-conversions/

Senior Housing News. (2023, October 18). *Why Transition Support Is Now a Must-Have for Senior Living*. Retrieved from https://seniorhousingnews.com/2023/10/18/why-transition-support-is-now-a-must-have-for-senior-living/

Senior Housing News. (2022, December 5). *To Sell Prospects on Value, Senior Living Operators Must Do Their Sales Homework*. Retrieved from https://seniorhousingnews.com/2022/12/05/to-sell-prospects-on-value-senior-living-operators-must-do-their-sales-homework/

U.S. Census Bureau. (2020). *Demographic Turning Points for the United States: Population Projections for 2020 to 2060*. Retrieved from https://www.census.gov

U.S. Census Bureau. (2023). *National Population Projections*. Retrieved from https://www.census.gov/data-tables/2023/demo/popproj/2023-summary-tables.html

U.S. Department of Health and Human Services, Administration for Community Living. (2023). *2023 Profile of Older Americans*. Retrieved from https://acl.gov/sites/default/files/Profile%20of%20OA/2023ProfileOlderAmericans.pdf

Ziegler. (2024). *Senior Living 2024 Outlook Report*. Retrieved from https://www.ziegler.com/z-media/7164/senior-living-2024-outlook.pdf

ABOUT THE AUTHOR

Kiera DesChamps is a connector, strategist, and advocate for aging adults navigating life transitions. With a professional foundation in counseling and over a decade of hands-on experience in the older adult living and move management industries, she brings a unique blend of emotional intelligence, logistical insight, and business acumen to her work.

Kiera is the founder of KD Consulting Group, where she partners with senior living operators, active adult communities, and sales professionals to transform their approach to occupancy, discovery, and client engagement. She is known for challenging the status quo—encouraging leaders to go beyond checklists and tours to truly understand the barriers that prevent prospects from moving forward.

With a background in higher education, professional move management, and strategic sales and business development, Kiera believes that the best outcomes happen when relationships are real, logistics are clear, and people are guided—not pressured—into their next chapter.

Whether she's training sales teams, supporting operators, or walking alongside families in transition, Kiera's work is grounded in empathy, practicality, and her unwavering belief that "where strategy meets success, connections create impact."

When she's not speaking, training, or building partnerships, Kiera finds joy in coaching others, creating community, and spending time with her husband Louis, who continues to cheer her on with love, patience, and unwavering support.

Connect with Kiera DesChamps

To book Kiera to speak at your organization, conference, or meeting:

Email: kd@kdconsults.com
Phone: 980-621-2199

Let's connect on social media:

LinkedIn:
https://www.linkedin.com/in/kieradeschamps

TikTok:
https://www.tiktok.com/@kdconsults

Instagram: @kdconsults

Website: www.kdconsults.com

If you are a fan of this book, please tell others...

- Write about *After the Tour* on your blog, e-magazine, company newsletter, and social media channels.
- Feature Kiera DesChamps as a keynote speaker, a guest on your podcast or radio/TV broadcast.
- Write an authentic, positive review on Amazon. com.
- Post on your social media channels.
- Purchase additional copies for your leadership team.